For **every child** across the globe,
YOU ARE **PRECIOUS**… YOU ARE **BEAUTIFUL**,
and this is just for you!

"No matter where your journeys take you, know that
you are beautiful & wonderfully created."
– **Patricia E. Lewis**

**Copyright © 2025 Patricia E. Lewis
All Rights Reserved.**

No part of this publication including text or illustrations
may be reproduced or stored in a retrieval system
or transmitted by any form or by any means,
electronic, mechanical, photocopying, recording or otherwise
without written permission of the publisher,
except in the context of brief quotations embodied in reviews.

This journal is intended for personal use only.
It is designed to serve as a resource and guide to help its users
experience with and practice positive journal writing.
Please consult with the appropriate professional if you have concerns
about yourself or your loved one's well-being.
The information contained within this journal may be helpful to many,
however, it should in no way substitute or replace therapy, counseling,
professional advice, or care. The publisher and author make no claims for
results and are not liable for the misuse of information contained herein.

For bulk purchases and educational discounts,
visit **www.jourdansjourneys.com**
or email **jourdansjourneys.series@gmail.com**

This Journal Belongs To

_____

With Love, From

_____

Date

_____

A Message to Me

May this journal be a *safe space*
to sort out my thoughts and feelings.

May the *thoughts* I allow my mind to
entertain help me focus on things that make me
strong, happy and proud of myself.

May this *focus* help to build my
self-esteem, self-image & self-confidence.

May the *positive words* I write here help me
find inner peace and happiness with
my abilities, uniqueness and divine design.

May my writing *journey* assist
me with removing negativity from my life.

May the *process* of journaling
help me to embrace the wonderful
things in and around me.

May these *wonderful things*
help me to help others in life.

CONTENTS

Journaling Benefits

Journaling Pages

a. Powerful Positivity

b. Freeform Journaling

Journaling Prompt Ideas

Positive Words & Affirmations Bank

Setting S.M.A.R.T. Goals

Jourdan's Journeys™

9 Journaling Benefits

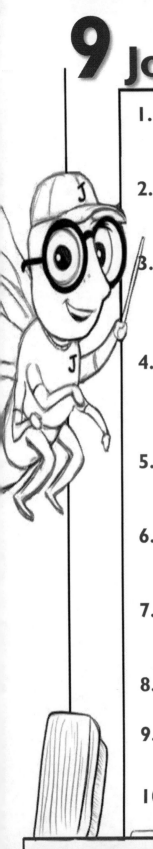

1. **Allows** me to express myself; a space for me to reflect

2. **Promotes** my focus by helping me process my feelings & emotions

3. **Engages** my brain; taps into my feelings, how I reason, and how I problem-solve; expands my imagination

4. **Helps** me to manage stress, unhappiness, and negative thinking; can enhance my happiness, mood and positive thoughts

5. **Boosts** my memory, comprehension and emotional intelligence

6. **Helps** me to track my goals whether personal, academic or professional

7. **Increases** the positive effects that are good for my physical health

8. **Enhances** my communication skills

9. **Encourages** thoughts about my future, things I want to do and places I want to go

10. **Other:**

Powerful Positivity

My opportunity to see the good in everything

S M T W T F S   Date: _____ Time: _____

Highlights of my day…
_____
_____

Positive words/affirmations about me today…
_____
_____

Things that made me feel special today…
_____
_____
_____

Things I am thankful for today…
_____
_____
_____

Things I learned about myself today…
_____
_____

"I am beautiful & wonderfully created."
– Jourdan's Journeys™

Today's Date _____ Time: _____

_____

_____

"Before I formed you in the womb I knew you,
before you were born I set you apart…"
– Jeremiah 1:5 (NIV)

Today's Date _____ Time: _____

"Your very existence is wrapped up in things you need to fulfill…remember the struggles along the way are only meant to shape you for your purpose." – *Chadwick Boseman*

Powerful Positivity

My opportunity to see the good in everything

S M T W T F S   Date: _____ Time: _____

Highlights of my day…
_____
_____

Positive words/affirmations about me today…
_____
_____

Things that made me feel special today…
_____
_____

Things I am thankful for today…
_____
_____

Things I learned about myself today…
_____
_____

"You are braver than you believe, stronger than you seem,
and smarter than you think."
— *Winnie the Pooh, Pooh's Most Grand Adventure*

Today's Date _____ Time: _____

"…if you have a goal, go for it, and if there is something in your way, just go around and find your path again, and go for your goal." – Quvenzhane Wallis

Today's Date _____ Time: _____

_____
_____
_____
_____
_____
_____
_____
_____
_____
_____
_____
_____
_____
_____
_____
_____
_____
_____
_____
_____
_____
_____
_____
_____
_____
_____
_____
_____
_____

"The best time to believe in yourself, even more,
is when it's not easy."
– Unknown

Powerful Positivity

My opportunity to see the good in everything

S M T W T F S   Date: _____ Time: _____

Highlights of my day…
_____
_____

Positive words/affirmations about me today…
_____
_____

Things that made me feel special today…
_____
_____
_____

Things I am thankful for today…
_____
_____
_____

Things I learned about myself today…
_____
_____

"Be strong and courageous. Do not be afraid;
do not be discouraged, for the Lord your God will be with
you wherever you go." – Joshua 1:9 (NIV)

Today's Date _____ Time: _____

_____
_____
_____
_____
_____
_____
_____
_____
_____
_____
_____
_____
_____
_____
_____
_____
_____
_____
_____
_____
_____
_____
_____
_____
_____
_____
_____

"…You can change everything that you have control over."
—Yara Shahidi

Today's Date _____ Time: _____

_____
_____

_____
_____
_____
_____
_____
_____
_____
_____
_____
_____
_____
_____
_____
_____
_____
_____
_____
_____
_____
_____
_____
_____
_____
_____

"…you've always got to believe in your heart that you've got what it takes to win it. You've always got to believe in yourself… You've always got to believe in the positives." – Lewis Hamilton

Powerful Positivity

My opportunity to see the good in everything

S M T W T F S   Date: _____ Time: _____

Highlights of my day…
_____
_____

Positive words/affirmations about me today…
_____
_____

Things that made me feel special today…
_____
_____
_____

Things I am thankful for today…
_____
_____
_____

Things I learned about myself today…
_____
_____

"Optimism is the faith that leads to achievement.
Nothing can be done without hope and confidence."
– Helen Keller

Today's Date _____ Time: _____

_____

_____

"I may be different, but that's okay. I like me."
— Jourdan's Journeys™

Today's Date _____ Time: _____

"Yet in all these things we are more than conquerors through Him who loved us."
– Romans 8:37 (NKJV)

Powerful Positivity
My opportunity to see the good in everything

S M T W T F S   Date: _____   Time: _____

Highlights of my day...
_____
_____

Positive words/affirmations about me today...
_____
_____

Things that made me feel special today...
_____
_____
_____

Things I am thankful for today...
_____
_____
_____

Things I learned about myself today...
_____
_____

"The flower that blooms in adversity is the
most rare and beautiful of all."
– Mulan

Today's Date _____   Time: _____

"You are a light. You are the light.
Never let anyone — any person or any force — dampen, dim
or diminish your light." – Senator John Lewis

Today's Date _____ Time: _____

"Every part of you is magnificent.
You are worthy of all the best things in life."
– Unknown

Powerful Positivity

My opportunity to see the good in everything

S M T W T F S   Date: _____ Time: _____

Highlights of my day…
_____
_____

Positive words/affirmations about me today…
_____
_____

Things that made me feel special today…
_____
_____
_____

Things I am thankful for today…
_____
_____
_____

Things I learned about myself today…
_____
_____

"In every thing give thanks: for this is the will of God
in Christ Jesus concerning you."
– I Thessalonians 5:18 (KJV)

Today's Date _____ Time: _____

"Have courage and be kind."
– Cinderella

Today's Date _____ Time: _____

_____

_____

_____

_____

_____

_____

_____

_____

_____

_____

_____

_____

_____

_____

_____

_____

_____

_____

_____

_____

_____

_____

_____

_____

_____

_____

_____

_____

"You have to believe in yourself when no one else does.
That makes you a winner right there."
—Venus Williams

Powerful Positivity

My opportunity to see the good in everything

S M T W T F S   Date: _____ Time: _____

Highlights of my day…
_____
_____

Positive words/affirmations about me today…
_____
_____

Things that made me feel special today…
_____
_____
_____

Things I am thankful for today…
_____
_____
_____

Things I learned about myself today…
_____
_____

"There's no prerequisites to worthiness. You're born worthy…"
–Viola Davis

Today's Date _____ Time: _____

"Don't be afraid to reach for the stars."
– Ellen Ochoa

Today's Date _____ Time: _____

"You must not let anyone define your limits
because of where you come from."
– Ratatouille

Powerful Positivity

My opportunity to see the good in everything

S M T W T F S   Date: _____ Time: _____

Highlights of my day…
_____
_____

Positive words/affirmations about me today…
_____
_____

Things that made me feel special today…
_____
_____
_____

Things I am thankful for today…
_____
_____
_____

Things I learned about myself today…
_____
_____

"Your uniqueness is what makes you shine."
– Unknown

Today's Date _____ Time: _____

_____

_____

"With faith, we can overcome anything."
— Jourdan's Journeys™

Today's Date _____ Time: _____

_____

_____

_____

"I can do all things through Christ who strengthens me."
— Philippians 4:13 (NKJV)

Powerful Positivity

My opportunity to see the good in everything

S M T W T F S   Date: _____ Time: _____

Highlights of my day...
_____
_____

Positive words/affirmations about me today...
_____
_____

Things that made me feel special today...
_____
_____
_____

Things I am thankful for today...
_____
_____
_____

Things I learned about myself today...
_____
_____

"When life gets you down, you know what you gotta do?
Just keep swimming." – Finding Nemo

Today's Date _____ Time: _____

"I can be changed by what happens to me.
But I refuse to be reduced by it."
– Maya Angelou

Today's Date _____ Time: _____

___

"The opinion which other people have of you
is their problem, not yours."
— Elisabeth Kubler-Ross

Powerful Positivity

My opportunity to see the good in everything

S M T W T F S   Date: _____ Time: _____

Highlights of my day…

_____
_____

Positive words/affirmations about me today…

_____
_____

Things that made me feel special today…

_____
_____
_____

Things I am thankful for today…

_____
_____
_____

Things I learned about myself today…

_____
_____

"The LORD your God has chosen you out of all the peoples on the face of the earth to be his people, his treasured possession." – Deuteronomy 7:6

Today's Date _____ Time: _____

"When anyone tells me I can't do anything,
I'm just not listening anymore."
– Florence Griffith Joyner

Today's Date _____ Time: _____

"I am what I am. I love me!...I love that God has allowed me to take whatever it was that I had and to make something out of it." – Stevie Wonder

Powerful Positivity

My opportunity to see the good in everything

S M T W T F S   Date: _____ Time: _____

Highlights of my day...
_____
_____

Positive words/affirmations about me today...
_____
_____

Things that made me feel special today...
_____
_____
_____

Things I am thankful for today...
_____
_____
_____

Things I learned about myself today...
_____
_____

"I am who I am and that is good enough."
– Jourdan's Journeys ™

Today's Date _____ Time: _____

"…I will fear no evil; For You are with me;
Your rod and Your staff, they comfort me."
– Psalm 23:4 (NKJV)

Today's Date _____ Time: _____

"For those who feel a little discouraged, you don't have to live at the top of the reef to be somebody."
– Shark Tale

Powerful Positivity
My opportunity to see the good in everything

S M T W T F S   Date: _____ Time: _____

Highlights of my day…
_____
_____

Positive words/affirmations about me today…
_____
_____

Things that made me feel special today…
_____
_____
_____

Things I am thankful for today…
_____
_____
_____

Things I learned about myself today…
_____
_____

"Nobody gets to live life backward.
Look ahead—that's where your future lies."
– Ann Landers

Today's Date _____ Time: _____

_____

_____

"Loving yourself is about understanding who you are, beyond your appearance, and it's what gives life to everything about you."
– Phylicia Rashad

Today's Date _____ Time: _____

"God is our refuge and strength, a very present help in trouble."
— Psalm 46:1 (KJV)

Powerful Positivity
My opportunity to see the good in everything

S M T W T F S   Date: _____ Time: _____

Highlights of my day…
_____
_____

Positive words/affirmations about me today…
_____
_____

Things that made me feel special today…
_____
_____
_____

Things I am thankful for today…
_____
_____
_____

Things I learned about myself today…
_____
_____

"When we prove to ourselves…what seemed impossible was just a self-imposed limitation caused by self doubt…"
– Alex Toussaint

Today's Date _____ Time: _____

"Be the change that you wish to see in the world."
– Mahatma Gandhi

Today's Date _____ Time: _____

"You must do the things you think you cannot do."
– Eleanor Roosevelt

Powerful Positivity

My opportunity to see the good in everything

S M T W T F S   Date: _____ Time: _____

Highlights of my day...

_____
_____

Positive words/affirmations about me today...

_____
_____

Things that made me feel special today...

_____
_____
_____

Things I am thankful for today...

_____
_____
_____

Things I learned about myself today...

_____
_____

"I will say of the Lord, He is my refuge and my fortress;
My God, in Him I will trust." – Psalm 91:2 (NKJV)

Today's Date _____ Time: _____

_____
_____

_____
_____
_____
_____
_____
_____
_____
_____
_____
_____
_____
_____
_____
_____
_____
_____
_____
_____
_____
_____
_____
_____
_____
_____
_____
_____
_____
_____
_____
_____
_____

"We all have a story to tell…
How are you going to tell your story?"
– Alena Analeigh (Wicker) McQuarter

Today's Date _____ Time: _____

_____
_____

"The best way to predict the future is to create it."
— Peter F. Drucker

Powerful Positivity
My opportunity to see the good in everything

S M T W T F S   Date: _____ Time: _____

Highlights of my day…

_____
_____

Positive words/affirmations about me today…

_____
_____

Things that made me feel special today…

_____
_____
_____

Things I am thankful for today…

_____
_____
_____

Things I learned about myself today…

_____
_____

"I will stay focused because I am in control of my future."
– Jourdan's Journeys™

Today's Date _____ Time: _____

_____

_____

"For you created my inmost being; you knit me together in my mother's womb… I am fearfully and wonderfully made; your works are wonderful, I know that full well." – Psalm 139:14 (NIV)

Today's Date _____ Time: _____

"I see now that the circumstances of one's birth are irrelevant. It is what you do with the gift of life that determines who you are." – Pokemon

Powerful Positivity

My opportunity to see the good in everything

S M T W T F S   Date: _____ Time: _____

Highlights of my day…

_____
_____

Positive words/affirmations about me today…

_____
_____

Things that made me feel special today…

_____
_____
_____

Things I am thankful for today…

_____
_____
_____

Things I learned about myself today…

_____
_____

"…be exactly who you are.
We are all a little different, and that's awesome!"
– Cole Blakeway

Today's Date _____ Time: _____

"It's said that God gave us fingerprints no one else has, so we can leave an imprint no one else can. Celebrate your originality — it's your greatest strength." – Gaur Gopal Das

Today's Date _____ Time: _____

"...Weeping may endure for a night,
But joy comes in the morning."
– Psalm 30:5 (NKJV)

Powerful Positivity

My opportunity to see the good in everything

S M T W T F S   Date: _____ Time: _____

Highlights of my day…

_____
_____

Positive words/affirmations about me today…

_____
_____

Things that made me feel special today…

_____
_____
_____

Things I am thankful for today…

_____
_____
_____

Things I learned about myself today…

_____
_____

"We are each other's harvest; we are each other's business;
we are each other's magnitude and bond."
— Gwendolyn Brooks

Today's Date _____ Time: _____

"Be more concerned with your character than your reputation, because character is what you really are, while your reputation is merely what others think you are." – Coach John Wooden

Today's Date _____ Time: _____

"I will help and not hinder others…
I can only do one 'H' at a time anyway."
– Jourdan's Journeys™

Powerful Positivity

My opportunity to see the good in everything

S M T W T F S   Date: _____ Time: _____

Highlights of my day…

_____
_____

Positive words/affirmations about me today…

_____
_____

Things that made me feel special today…

_____
_____
_____

Things I am thankful for today…

_____
_____
_____

Things I learned about myself today…

_____

"These things I have spoken to you, that in Me you may have peace. In the world you will have tribulation; but be of good cheer…" – John 16:33 (NKJV)

Today's Date _____ Time: _____

_____
_____
_____

"I need to see my own beauty and to continue to be reminded that I am enough, that I am worthy of love without effort, that I am beautiful,… worthy and okay."
– Tracee Ellis Ross

Today's Date _____ Time: _____

_____

_____

"Your success will be determined by your own confidence and fortitude."
— Michelle Obama

Powerful Positivity
My opportunity to see the good in everything

S M T W T F S   Date: _____ Time: _____

Highlights of my day…
_____
_____

Positive words/affirmations about me today…
_____
_____

Things that made me feel special today…
_____
_____
_____

Things I am thankful for today…
_____
_____
_____

Things I learned about myself today…
_____
_____

"Believing in your dreams is the first step towards
turning them into reality."
– Unknown

Today's Date _____ Time: _____

_____
_____
_____
_____
_____
_____
_____
_____
_____
_____
_____
_____
_____
_____
_____
_____
_____
_____
_____
_____
_____
_____
_____
_____
_____
_____
_____
_____
_____

"Start where you are with what you have. You are enough."
– Germany Kent

Today's Date _____ Time: _____

_____

_____

"Now, think of the happiest things.
It's the same as having wings!"
– Peter Pan

Powerful Positivity

My opportunity to see the good in everything

S M T W T F S   Date:_____ Time:_____

Highlights of my day…
_____
_____

Positive words/affirmations about me today…
_____
_____

Things that made me feel special today…
_____
_____
_____

Things I am thankful for today…
_____
_____
_____

Things I learned about myself today…
_____
_____

"Self-love, self-respect, self-worth…there is a reason they all start with 'self'. You cannot find them in anyone else."
– Unknown

Today's Date _____ Time: _____

_____
_____

"A winner is a dreamer who never gives up."
– Nelson Mandela

Today's Date _____ Time: _____

"In all your ways acknowledge Him, And He shall direct your paths." – Proverbs 3:6 (NKJV)

Powerful Positivity

My opportunity to see the good in everything

S M T W T F S   Date: _____ Time: _____

Highlights of my day…
_____
_____

Positive words/affirmations about me today…
_____
_____

Things that made me feel special today…
_____
_____
_____

Things I am thankful for today…
_____
_____
_____

Things I learned about myself today…
_____
_____

"I will only compete against myself…I will never give up."
— Jourdan's Journeys™

Today's Date _____ Time: _____

"Find something you love to do.
You'll know it's right when you find something that
benefits humanity in it." – Piece by Piece

Today's Date _____ Time: _____

"So do not throw away your confidence;… You need to persevere so that when you have done the will of God, you will receive what he has promised." – Hebrews 10:35–36 (NIV)

Powerful Positivity

My opportunity to see the good in everything

S M T W T F S   Date: _____ Time: _____

Highlights of my day…

_____
_____

Positive words/affirmations about me today…

_____
_____

Things that made me feel special today…

_____
_____
_____

Things I am thankful for today…

_____
_____
_____

Things I learned about myself today…

_____
_____

"You can't change destiny. Change your fate."
– Brave

Today's Date _____ Time: _____

_____

_____

"Success is a journey, not a destination.
The doing is often more important than the outcome."
– Arthur Ashe

Today's Date _____ Time: _____

"Trust in the Lord with all your heart, and do not trust in your own understanding."
— Proverbs 3:5 (NLV)

Powerful Positivity

My opportunity to see the good in everything

S M T W T F S   Date: _____ Time: _____

Highlights of my day…
_____
_____

Positive words/affirmations about me today…
_____
_____

Things that made me feel special today…
_____
_____
_____

Things I am thankful for today…
_____
_____
_____

Things I learned about myself today…
_____
_____

"Be as bold as the first man or (woman) to eat an oyster."
– Shirley Chisholm

Today's Date _____ Time: _____

Math 101
Impossible = I'm possible

Today's Date _____ Time: _____

"I always tell young people to hold on to their dreams. And sometimes you have to stand up for what you think is right even if you have to stand alone." – Claudette Colvin

Powerful Positivity

My opportunity to see the good in everything

S M T W T F S   Date: _____ Time: _____

Highlights of my day…
_____
_____

Positive words/affirmations about me today…
_____
_____

Things that made me feel special today…
_____
_____
_____

Things I am thankful for today…
_____
_____
_____

Things I learned about myself today…
_____
_____

"The Lord is my light and my salvation; whom shall I fear?
the Lord is the strength of my life;
of whom shall I be afraid?" – Psalm 27:1 (KJV)

Today's Date _____   Time: _____

_____

_____

_____

_____

_____

_____

_____

_____

_____

_____

_____

_____

_____

_____

_____

_____

_____

_____

_____

_____

_____

_____

_____

_____

_____

"In this world, I will not fear… I will not be afraid.
I can, I am, and I will."
– Jourdan's Journeys™

Today's Date _____ Time: _____

_____
_____

"You are one of one. None before and none to come.
That what makes you different, makes you beautiful."
– Pharrell Williams

Powerful Positivity

My opportunity to see the good in everything

S M T W T F S   Date: _____ Time: _____

Highlights of my day...

_____
_____

Positive words/affirmations about me today...

_____
_____

Things that made me feel special today...

_____
_____

Things I am thankful for today...

_____
_____

Things I learned about myself today...

_____
_____

"It's not what others think,
it's what you think about yourself that counts." – Unknown

Today's Date _____ Time: _____

"But blessed is the one who trusts in the LORD, whose confidence is in him." – Jeremiah 17:7 (NIV)

Today's Date _____ Time: _____

"The only thing that matters is what you choose to be now."
– Kung Fu Panda

Powerful Positivity
My opportunity to see the good in everything

S M T W T F S   Date: _____ Time: _____

Highlights of my day…
_____
_____

Positive words/affirmations about me today…
_____
_____

Things that made me feel special today…
_____
_____
_____

Things I am thankful for today…
_____
_____
_____

Things I learned about myself today…
_____
_____

"I feel very strongly about making peace and love in the world."
– Ella Jenkins

Today's Date _____ Time: _____

"The most important thing is God's blessing…if you believe in God and you believe in yourself, you have nothing to worry about."
– Denzel Hayes Washington, Jr.

Today's Date _____ Time: _____

"Fear not, for I am with you; Be not dismayed, for I am your God.
I will strengthen you, Yes, I will help you…"
– Isaiah 41:10 (NKJV)

Powerful Positivity

My opportunity to see the good in everything

S M T W T F S   Date: _____ Time: _____

Highlights of my day...
_____
_____

Positive words/affirmations about me today...
_____
_____

Things that made me feel special today...
_____
_____
_____

Things I am thankful for today...
_____
_____
_____

Things I learned about myself today...
_____
_____

"You can't focus on what's going wrong.
There's always a way to turn things around." - Inside Out

Today's Date _____ Time: _____

"There's an "I" in Life." – Unknown

Today's Date _____ Time: _____

"What God intended for you goes far beyond anything you can imagine." – Oprah Winfrey

Powerful Positivity

My opportunity to see the good in everything

S M T W T F S   Date: _____ Time: _____

Highlights of my day…
_____
_____

Positive words/affirmations about me today…
_____
_____

Things that made me feel special today…
_____
_____
_____

Things I am thankful for today…
_____
_____
_____

Things I learned about myself today…
_____
_____

"Remember who you are…"
–The Lion King

Today's Date _____ Time: _____

_____
_____
_____
_____
_____
_____
_____
_____
_____
_____
_____
_____
_____
_____
_____
_____
_____
_____
_____
_____
_____
_____
_____
_____
_____
_____
_____
_____
_____

"To excel at the highest level - or any level, really - you need to believe in yourself,…"
—Wardell Stephen Curry II

Today's Date _____ Time: _____

_____

_____

"Use me, God. Show me how to take who I am, who I want to be, and what I can do, and use it for a purpose greater than myself." – Dr. Martin Luther King Jr.

Powerful Positivity
My opportunity to see the good in everything

S M T W T F S   Date: _____ Time: _____

Highlights of my day…
_____
_____

Positive words/affirmations about me today…
_____
_____

Things that made me feel special today…
_____
_____
_____

Things I am thankful for today…
_____
_____
_____

Things I learned about myself today…
_____
_____

"Practice creates confidence. Confidence empowers you."
– Simone Biles

Today's Date _____ Time: _____

_____

_____

_____
_____
_____
_____
_____
_____
_____
_____
_____
_____
_____
_____
_____
_____
_____
_____
_____
_____
_____
_____
_____
_____
_____
_____
_____
_____
_____
_____

"Every individual makes a difference and you have to decide what kind of difference you want to make."
– Jane Goodall (born Valerie Jane Morris-Goodall)

Today's Date _____ Time: _____

There's a "ME" in MEaningful!
– Unknown

Powerful Positivity

My opportunity to see the good in everything

S M T W T F S   Date: _____ Time: _____

Highlights of my day…
_____
_____

Positive words/affirmations about me today…
_____
_____

Things that made me feel special today…
_____
_____
_____

Things I am thankful for today…
_____
_____
_____

Things I learned about myself today…
_____
_____

"There's nothing I can't do without the help of God, my family, and my village." – Jourdan's Journeys™

Today's Date _____ Time: _____

"Courage is not about knowing the path, it's about taking the first step." – Katie Davis Majors

Today's Date _____ Time: _____

"Keep exploring. Keep dreaming. Keep asking why. Don't settle for what you already know. Never stop believing in the power of your ideas, your imagination, your hard work to change the world." – President Barack Obama

Powerful Positivity

My opportunity to see the good in everything

S M T W T F S   Date: _____ Time: _____

Highlights of my day…

_____

_____

Positive words/affirmations about me today…

_____

_____

Things that made me feel special today…

_____

_____

_____

Things I am thankful for today…

_____

_____

_____

Things I learned about myself today…

_____

_____

"For God hath not given us the spirit of fear; but of power,
and of love, and of a sound mind."
– 2 Timothy 1:7 (KJV)

Today's Date _____ Time: _____

_____
_____

_____
_____
_____
_____
_____
_____
_____
_____
_____
_____
_____
_____
_____
_____
_____
_____
_____
_____
_____
_____
_____
_____
_____
_____
_____
_____
_____
_____

"You are never too old to set another goal
or to dream a new dream."
– Malala Yousafzai

Today's Date _____   Time: _____

Math 101
"I am the product of my thoughts multiplied by my actions."
– Unknown

Powerful Positivity

My opportunity to see the good in everything

S M T W T F S   Date: _____ Time: _____

Highlights of my day…
_____
_____

Positive words/affirmations about me today…
_____
_____

Things that made me feel special today…
_____
_____
_____

Things I am thankful for today…
_____
_____
_____

Things I learned about myself today…
_____
_____

"I don't care who is doing better than me… It's me vs me."
– Michael Bakari Jordan

Today's Date _____ Time: _____

"And he shall be like a tree planted by the rivers of water, that bringeth forth his fruit in his season; his leaf also shall not wither; and whatsoever he doeth shall prosper." – Psalm 1:3

Today's Date _____ Time: _____

_____

_____

"My word is my bond; integrity is all you have."
— Malcolm-Jamal Warner

Today's Date _____ Time: _____

"…I know God has a plan for me."
– Zharnel Hughes

Journaling Prompt Ideas

Just in case I need some inspiration, I will use one of these writing prompts to get me going… **happy writing to me!**

1. Describe 3 positive words about me. What do these words mean and why do they represent me?

2. List 3 things I like about myself. Why are these things special to me?

3. Write an affirmation to encourage myself. Why is that affirmation important to me? How will I apply the affirmation to my everyday life?

4. Write about something that makes me feel special or unique. Why does it make me feel this way?

Journaling Prompt Ideas

5. Write about something that made me smile or made me happy. Why did it make me smile or happy?

6. List one thing I did that made me proud of myself. Why did it make me feel proud?

7. Write about the facial expression I circled in my "feelings" tracker today. Why did I choose that expression today?

8. Write about something I learned today. How does learning new things make me feel?

9. List one thing I am thankful for, even if it seems small. Why am I thankful for this?

Journaling Prompt Ideas

10. Write a positive affirmation about myself. I must **Write it… Say it… and Believe it!**

11. Think about a time when I felt frustrated or sad. What is something good or a lesson I learned in that moment although it did not feel good?

12. Describe a time when I chose to be brave. Why did I choose to be brave and what did I learn about myself?

13. Describe something nice I did for someone or something nice someone did for me. How did it make me feel?

14. Who is someone I admire, and what do I like most about them?

Journaling Prompt Ideas

15. What positive qualities do I want others to admire and realize in me? Am I currently exemplifying or demonstrating these qualities? How do others know I possess these qualities? How do these qualities help me and how do these same qualities help other people?

16. What unique skills and/or abilities do I have that makes me stand out from others? What is my unique beauty? How can I share my unique beauty with others in a positive way?

17. List one or more positive things I am looking forward to tomorrow. How does the excitement make me feel?

Journaling Prompt Ideas

18. List one **very short-term goal** (0 to 6 weeks). How will I accomplish this goal? Who and what tools if any, do I need to help me accomplish my goal? When would I like to accomplish my goal? How will accomplishing this goal make me feel?

19. List one **short-term goal** (6 weeks to 3 months). Answer questions found in #18.

20. List one **mid-term goal** (3 months to 6 months). Answer questions found in #18.

21. List one **long-term goal** (6 months to 12 months). Answer questions found in #18.

22. List one **longer-term goal** that stretches beyond 1 year. Answer questions found in #18.

Journaling Prompt Ideas

23. Go back to one of my goals. How am I progressing with that goal? Did I reach the goal? If yes, how does that make me feel?
If not, what has changed? Answer questions in #18 if this goal is still important to me.

24. Repeat. Find a new goal to set, write about and achieve.

25. Write about a goal I have already achieved. What made that goal possible for me to achieve? How can I apply the success of that goal to other areas in my life?

26. Select a word from "My Positive Words & Affirmations Bank". Describe how this word and affirmation applies to my everyday life.

Special Note: Learn about the importance of setting goals in the **Setting S.M.A.R.T. Goals** section at the end of this journal.

My Positive Words & Affirmations Bank

I will use these words & affirmations to remind me of how **beautiful & wonderfully created I AM**.

I AM	Affirmation
Authentic	"I am true to myself, rare and genuine. I will be me and no one else."
Beautiful	"I love my unique beauty and celebrate the beauty in others."
Brave	"I will not be afraid to face challenges in my life."
Bright	"I am intelligent and smart."
Brilliant	"I have an active mind and will excel at many things in life."
Calm	"I will be focused and relaxed even in stressful situations."
Capable	"I am competent and able to handle different tasks."

My Positive Words & Affirmations Bank

I AM	Affirmation
Confident	"I believe in myself."
Courageous	"I will face my fears even when a little uncomfortable."
Creative	"I will use my creativity to learn, have fun and work through any challenges in my life."
Delightful	"I welcome today with a pleasant outlook on life."
Deserving	"I am worthy of good things, people and experiences."
Determined	"Nothing will stop me. I will succeed in all that I do."
Dynamic	"I am multifaceted and the driving force behind the positivity in my life."

My Positive Words & Affirmations Bank

I AM	Affirmation
Educated	"I will learn each day to get the knowledge I need for my life."
Ethical	"I will exercise good morals & principles through my actions."
Excellent	"I have the ability to be excellent in the areas I choose."
Expressive	"I will express myself through healthy art forms like writing."
Extravagant	"I am not afraid to stand out from others and be different."
Fearless	"I will be bold, and courageous to help me face my fears."
Forgiving	"I will forgive others. Forgiveness is for me first."

My Positive Words & Affirmations Bank

I AM	Affirmation
Genuine	"I will be sincere and authentic in my words and actions."
Gifted	"I am naturally talented. I will use my talents to help others."
Grateful	"I will accept and appreciate the many blessings in my life."
Grounded	"I will focus to overcome challenges in my life, with help when needed."
Happy	"I will do my best to find joy and happiness everyday."
Hardworking	"I will work smart and put in the effort to achieve my goals."
Honest	"I will remain true to myself and others."

My Positive Words & Affirmations Bank

I AM	Affirmation
Honorable	"I have integrity and will always strive to do what is right and just."
Inquisitive	"I will be a curious learner and ask questions to gain knowledge."
Intelligent	"I am capable of grasping new ideas and applying them to my life."
Natural	"I have natural, God-given abilities and talents."
Open-Minded	"I will respect the opinions of others even when I disagree.
Optimistic	"I will be positive and find ways to see the good in my experiences."
Original	"I am unique & special. I will share my uniqueness with the world."

My Positive Words & Affirmations Bank

I AM	Affirmation
Patient	"I will accept delays and challenges in my life. I will wait calmly without becoming upset or anxious."
Persistent	"When times get rough, I will not give up. I will pursue my plans and goals even during times of difficulty or adversity."
Positive	"I will focus on the good and finding solutions to problems."
Powerful	"I will make a significant impact in the world."
Radiant	"I am a star! I will light up my environment with positive energy."
Reflective	"I will take time to think about my experiences and learn from them."

My Positive Words & Affirmations Bank

I AM	Affirmation
Resilient	"I will do my best to turn negative experiences into positive moments."
Self-Assured	"I am self-assured and confident, believing in myself and my abilities."
Self-Confident	"I am able to face new challenges with a positive mindset."
Self-Disciplined	"I will stay on track to achieve my goals in life."
Serene	"I will protect my mind with a calm and relaxing attitude."
Smart	"I have the ability to learn quickly and excel in various areas."

My Positive Words & Affirmations Bank

I AM	Affirmation
Spiritual	"My creation has meaning and purpose beyond this world."
Strong	"My mind is strong. I will not let peer pressure take me away from the positive things I put my mind to do."
Successful	"My goals and aspirations belong to me. I will determine what is meaningful and define what success looks like to me."
Talented	"I am skilled at performing and achieving tasks with excellence."
Tenacious	"I am persistent and will never give up on my goals and dreams."
Tough	"I am able to overcome challenges with strength and determination."

My Positive Words & Affirmations Bank

I AM	Affirmation
Unique	"I am original, one of a kind. I am unlike anyone else."
Versatile	"I will use my talents and abilities often. I will not hide these gifts."
Vital	"I am important! I matter to this world and those around me."
Wholesome	"I will do what is right by practicing strong morals & ethics."
Wonderful	"I will use my personality to bring joy and happiness to others."
Youthful	"No matter my age, I will use my energy and curiosity to explore the world around me."
Zealous	"Nothing will stop me from reaching my goals in life."

My Positive Words & Affirmations Bank

(with room for me to write my own below)

I AM	Affirmation

Setting Goals

My goals are the **future** desired **results or achievements** that I plan to work towards. They can be **big or small** and used in my **everyday life**. Goals help me to stay on track with the things that are **most important to me.**

S.M.A.R.T. Goals

My goals should follow these simple rules:

S – *Specific:* clearly state what I want to achieve

M – *Measurable:* track & check my progress often

A – *Achievable:* my goal is within my reach of achieving

R – *Relevant:* my goal is important and applies to me

T – *Time-bound:* my goal has a set deadline for achieving

Once my goals are achieved, I can decide if I need to repeat the accomplishment or consider a new goal.

S.M.A.R.T. Examples

- I will learn to tie my shoelaces by the time I am 6 years old by practicing to tie them twice everyday.
- I will walk my dog twice a day for 10 minutes each time.
- I will play my instrument for 1 hour every week.
- I will exercise by walking at least 17 days each month.
- I will save $25 a month to buy a new Lego set next year.

Jourdan's Journeys™

Other books in the
Jourdan's Journeys™ book series
can be found at your favorite
online bookstore

For Jourdan merchandise, visit
www.jourdansjourneys.com

Tag and follow Jourdan on Social Media:

@Jourdans Journeys

@Jourdans_Journeys

@jourdansjourneys

"You are the author of your life.
Tell your story the way
only you can." – Unknown